D1104065

By Laura Williams
Translated by Albana Hoxha

© 2022 Williams Books
1 rue de l'église, 91430 Igny
Dépôt légal : Décembre 2022
ISBN 978-2-492960-98-7
Imprimé à la demande par Amazon
Loi n° 49-956 du 16 juillet 1949 sur les publications destinées à la jeunesse

aeroplan

airplane

mollë

apple

avokado

avocado

fëmijë

baby

topi
ball

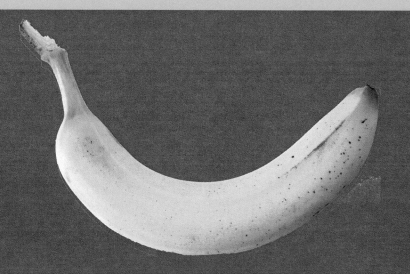

banane
banana

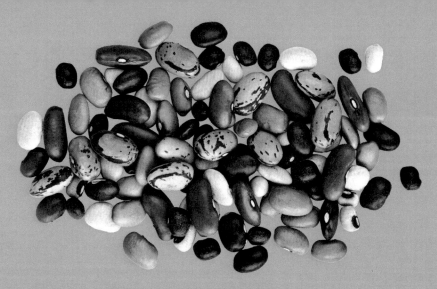

fasule

beans

ariu

bear

shtrat

bed

bleta

bee

biciklete

bike

zog

bird

varkë

boat

libër

book

shishe

bottle

tas

bowl

bukë

bread

flutur

butterfly

makinë

car

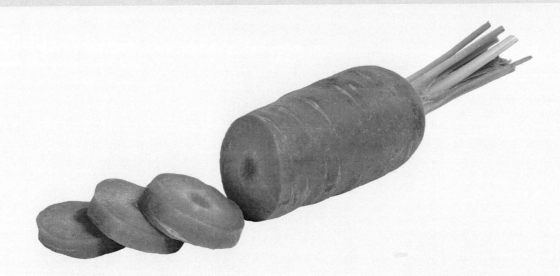

karrota

carrot

macja

cat

karrige

chair

djathë
cheese

pulë
chicken

ora

clock

re

cloud

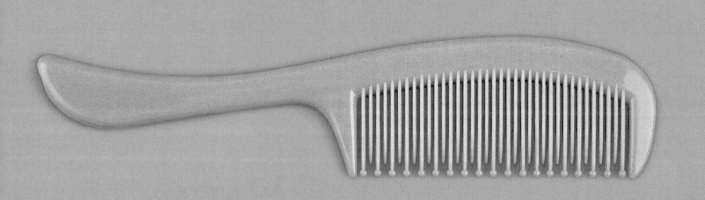

krehër

comb

misër

corn

lopë
cow

qeni
dog

dera

door

rosë

duck

vezë

egg

elefant

elephant

peshku

fish

lule

flower

bretkocë

frog

gjirafë

giraffe

dorë

hand

kapelë

hat

kalë

horse

shtëpi

house

lëng

juice

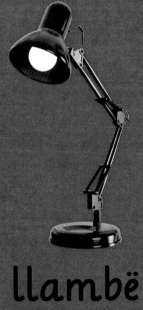

llambë

lamp

gjethe

leaf

luani

lion

qumësht

milk

pasqyrë

mirror

majmun

monkey

mali

mountain

fole

nest

vaj

oil

pikturë

painting

letër

paper

papagall

parrot

perlat

pearls

derr

pig

pëllumb

pigeon

ananasi

pineapple

pjatë

plate

patate

potato

radio

radio

shiu

rain

ylber

rainbow

oriz

rice

rrugë

road

litar

rope

thes

sack

sallatë

salad

kripë

salt

rërë

sand

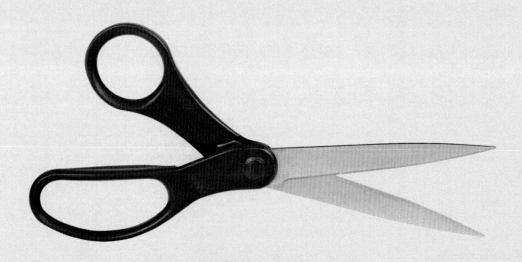

gërshërët

scissors

këpucët

shoes

qielli

sky

gjarpër

snake

sapun

soap

çorape

socks

lugë

spoon

yll
star

guri
stone

sheqer

sugar

dielli

sun

tavolinë

table

lavaman

tap

çaj

tea

televizori

television

tendë

tent

domate

tomato

gjuha

tongue

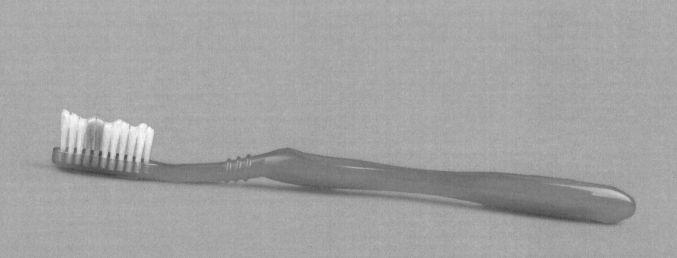

furçë dhëmbësh

toothbrush

treni

train

pemë

tree

kamion

truck

breshkë

turtle

çadër

umbrella

mur

wall

grerëz

wasp

ujë

water

druri

wood

zebër

zebra

Thank you

I just wanted to thank you for purchasing this book. You are assisting my work, for which I am extremely grateful.

The best way to support me is through a review on Amazon. Your feedback assists me in better understanding your needs.
It also helps me to create and publish more books that will support the learning of bilingual children of all ages.

Thank you in advance for your help.

You can scan the following QR code or go to the link below to access the reviews on Amazon.

https://www.amazon.com/review/create-review?&asin=2492960986

In the same collection

Albanian - English Words for Toddlers

Action Verbs

Laura Williams

Albanian - English Words for Toddlers

Fruits and Vegetables

Laura Williams

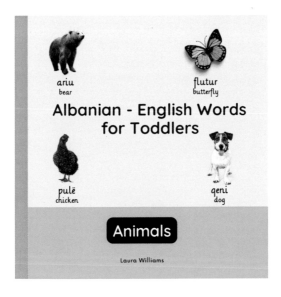

Albanian - English Words for Toddlers

Animals

Laura Williams

Made in United States
North Haven, CT
12 April 2023

35338021R00031